COME FLY WITH ME

by

Mary Foster

DIAMOND MEDIA PRESS CO.
1-304-460-1427
https://www.diamondmediapressco.com/

Copyright © 2023

By **Mary Foster**
All rights reserved.

ISBN Paperback: 978-1-7333011-3-8

Introduction

Hi my name Is Mary Foster now, but I have had five last names over the last 57 years. The first last name was Brabbs, this is my maiden name. I kept going back to the name I had the longest. I started out as Mary Brabbs, that was the name I grew up with. Then I married a man named Mark Foster, I was married to him for eighteen years, that's one year longer than I was single. My second married name was Vallett, I had that name for four years. My third married name was Perry, that name lasted nine years. Then the last name was Sandoval, this was really short, it lasted ten months. Seeing how I was a Foster for eighteen years it just seems natural that I would cling to that name. Now that I have introduce myself officially, I would like to invite you into my world and inform you of all the ups and downs that my life contained and how I have not allowed these downs to get the best of me. To show you what place sure determination played trough out my life, and to let you know that there is nothing that replaces determination.

CHAPTER 1
My Childhood

Being brought up in a catholic school

I grew up in a family of five children, in what would be known today as a large family. I had an older sister, an older brother and two younger brothers. Yes, I was the middle child.

I wasn't born into a God fearing Catholic family but soon after I started elementary (after kindergarten I believe) my mom became Catholic, my dad never did. My brothers, sister and I followed my mom example and the five of us became Catholic too (not that we were given any choice). I went to a public school for kindergarten, I don't remember that teacher's name but the one thing I do remember is getting spanked for going into the boy's bathroom. After we became Catholic I went to a Catholic elementary school in which I excelled. I had a nun my first grade whose name was Sister Marie. I thought that nuns were really strict even though I didn't have any teachers to compare her with seeing how she was my first teacher. Because I excelled I loved school. I soon found out that all teachers in Catholic schools were not nuns or priests. In the second grade I was I had a teacher by a woman who was not a nun, named Becky Decker. The fact that I looked up to her so much gave me the idea that I wanted to be a teacher (this is how I felt in the second grade). I know second grade is kind of early to decide what you want to be but then that was my life long dream. In the third grade I had a really strict teacher whose name was Mrs. Ahern, I though the nun I had in the first grade was strict but Mrs. Ahern was really strict! Looking back on how strict she was now that I am an adult, I realize she had one of the toughest grades to teach. She had to teach writing, she had to make sure the student's penmanship was legible plus she had to teach all subjects. Fourth grade I had yet another teacher who was not a nun, Mrs. Luna, she was fun. Then in the fifth and sixth grade was a nun called Sister Bernardo. After being told that nuns primarily taught in Catholic schools, I just assumed this to be the case but in my first six years of school I had two nuns as teachers, first, fifth and sixth grade (fifth and sixth grade was the same nun).

My sister and I took a trip to Alaska from Michigan, between grades fourth and fifth grade, with my Aunt Betty who was living up there. We drove to Anchorage, Alaska from Flint, Michigan, which took us a total of six days. My aunt tried to make it an educational trip so she had my sister and I calculate the gas mileage as we traveled. I spent my eleventh birthday in Alaska, it was very memorable because my birthday is July 20 and the year was 1969, the day the men walked on the moon the first time. So you see my birthday went down in history books, how many people can say that? Both my mom's sister and brother lived in Anchorage, Alaska so we had Aunt Betty and Uncle Eddie trying to show us things a child would love to do with a little bit of Alaska thrown in. My Uncle Eddie took us fishing and my sister did really good, me not so good. My uncle believed you catch them, you eat them. You know I learned to hate fish that summer! Another event that I will always remember is when we went swimming at a lake, I learned that you never horse play on a raft in the middle of the lake, as I did and almost drowned that summer because I could not swim. So I learned two things that summer, to hate fish and be fearful of water.

Tragedy strikes

My life was forever changed when I was only twelve years old. My mother was very ill, so ill that she went into the emergency room help. She was told that there was a nursing strike and they wanted to keep her but there were no beds or physical nursing help so they told her to come back tomorrow. I was allowed to stay home from school to be with her that day. My mom was always concerned with her mom's well being, she lived next door to us. My mom walked over to my grandmother's house to fix her insulin. She collapsed on my grandmother's floor. My grandmother's landlord came over to get me while at the same time he sent someone down to the parking lot where my dad worked. I went into my grandmother's home before the paramedics got there to see my mom on the floor with her eyes rolled back where you could only see the whites, a sight I will never forget. My dad got there shortly after the paramedics did, he rode in the ambulance to the hospital with mom. When my dad returned home he broke the tragic news **my mom had died!** My family had a lot to comprehend. My mother, who was 33, had a pulmonary embolism, and a blood clot in her leg had broken away and traveled to her heart, I later found that she had to of had a rare genetic disease that all my brothers and sister have.

It was really strange to have people who had known you all of your life to be dumbfounded, not to know what to say to you. I remember looking up to God for help, when I noticed how the sky looked. The sunshine separated the white wispy clouds as if the gates of heaven were opening up to welcoming my mom home. It was after seeing that I knew that my mom would be fine. People could not understand but my mom and I understood.

Meeting my adopted mom

My father was given ten years to live by the doctors because of his emphysema, a disease he had contracted through his smoking and his line of work. My father had a bowling buddy, Ralph, who my father told of his concerns of not having anyone to watch his children while he was in the hospital (and he spent a lot of time in the hospital after my mom died). Ralph and his wife, Joy, volunteered their services. Joy played an important part in my life and any little girl age 12 needs a mother or a mother substitute. Although she played a big part in my life, I like to think I brought her just as much happiness but I think I got the better end of the deal.

Ralph and Joy had seven children of their own. The seven childrens ages were quite close to my siblings and my own age. Then there were the set of twin girls who were just infants when we entered into their lives. You would think that when we all got together we caused quite a commotion, well let me tell you we did but Joy loved it. Joy tells me that we brought some of her best memories to cherish. We did some activities that we had never done before, or would have done, my mom was gone my mom planned all our fun activities.

There is a couple things that I really remember well, one of the activities that I remember is when we would go to Cedar Point which is an amusement park in Ohio. We would convince Ralph and Joy to go with us on the log/water ride. Now Ralph and Joy are both large, heavy people, and we knew we would really get splashed with them sitting in front of this ride.

The other activity that comes to mind other than Cedar Point and that was when we were going to Greenfield Village in Michigan. I remember this so well because Joy had dressed us all in green. She went to pay for us and she told the woman that after the the last child dressed in green has gone through stop charging her.

We also took trips to Frankenmuth Michigan for dinner. Frankenmuth was famous for their chicken dinners. We used to rent out the whole dining room we would have Joy's seven kids, the five of us and sometimes we would take grandmothers and cousins. We really had a blast. Then after leaving we would watch the glockenspiel, which is a German clock with figurines that told a story. After we would watch this we would all go to Bronners, which is a Christmas store open year round. Joy and I both loved the season of Christmas with all the decorations, lights and smells. I have never changed my feeling about Christmas and I hope I never do.

My older brother James and I sort of followed what Ralph was so good at, which was bowling. Ralph bowled many perfect games of 300. James and I had joined a bowling league during the summer that I was 15 years old. In that league I bowled a 188. This was just a start of the different activities I was involved in that Ralph and Joy's influence had on me that was so strong. Even to this day I bowl, I bowl in three different leagues.

Joy was a very good mother substitution, she was a grandma to my children, she was always there when I needed her, she helped me through all my divorces. I lost my best friend(my adopted mom) sometime in August of 2012.

An Escape

Now as I grew older and we moved to Mount Morris, Michigan all childhood fun had stopped. I was now old enough to stay home by myself and watch my two younger brothers, we did not stay with Joy and Ralph as much as we used to. All the expectations of an adult woman were shifted to me. After all my older sister was off to college (thanks to Joy's ability to talk my father into letting her go to college) and my older brother and my father did not get along to well, so naturally expectations would have fallen on me. So I was an instant "mom/substitute wife", which I was not to keen on this idea. I knew that if I wanted to go to college it would be very hard because my dad would tell me all the reasons he needed me there and I would have folded and stayed.

I met this 21-year-old man, he was the son of my boss, the only man I had ever met who was of legal age. My boss was ill in October 1975 so I went over to visit her and I met her son who looked like a dream come true. I stayed a few hours and before I left I checked with her son to see if he would be there and that is how I determined when my next visit would be. His name was Mark. Mark was fresh out of the Air Force, when I met him he had only been home for a few weeks. We dated exclusively for four months starting in December 1975 and he asked me to marry him in March. The problem was I was only 17 and my father would have to sign a document saying that it was with his blessing that I could get married. Of course being my father's favorite child helped that aspect out; after all I had done everything my father had wanted me to do for five years. I told myself I was madly in love with Mark, but I was 17 and I don't think I knew what love was. Since I grew up Catholic I wanted to be married Catholic but the priest told me the only way we could get marred Catholic is if Mark would raise our children Catholic, I could not request that of Mark since he was not Catholic. Mark, although he was an adult was afraid of what his mother would say. You see I came from the wrong side of the tracks; I was not good enough for her son. So consequently Mark had said we should wait until his parents went on vacation, so we were married on April 16, 1976. We were married in a small Lutheran church, the only place we could find on such short notice seeing how it was Good Friday. We were married six weeks before I graduated from high school.

CHAPTER 2

The love of my life And The Accident

Yes, we got married six weeks before I graduated from high school. Mark did not have a job but we were happy. We were happy and we lived in a small one-bedroom apartment with a small puppy, which we were not supposed to have. Mark got a job training others how to exercise and how to get the best results out of their exercise. He was making money, it may not have been his dream job, but it was a job. We had periodically been looking at mobile homes and finally found the right one. It was big enough and it allowed dogs. We were extremely happy so after five weeks in this apartment that didn't allow dogs we decided that we should get a mobile home where we could have a dog. We were on the way to get a loan approved for this mobile home when tragedy struck.

Yes, tragedy once again struck my life, a different type of tragedy but tragedy just the same. While we were driving on Clio Road in Flint, Michigan, both of us being deliriously happy with no worries, Mark ran a red light and our car was broadsided. The car we were driving in was struck on my side by a pick-up truck. Causing whiplash in my brain. This is a day that changed my life forever which happened on May 25,1976. The car looked like an accordion. My head struck the side window, I had whiplash in my brain. For the longest time I felt like God was punishing me for not getting married Catholic, but Mark had mononucleosis which caused him to miss the fact that the light was red. This is what I told myself for 18 years, but today I realize it was just **that** an accident because two kids were so happy they weren't paying attention.

Death and Feeling free
seeing my mom

In this car accident I died and when I died I saw my mom in a blinding white light. Now remember she had died five and a half years earlier. At that moment I was so happy to see her, I felt so free, I knew that she would set my father straight. All I wanted was to go with her and see what her new home was like. To my dismay she told me to go back, it was not yet my time, I had much to do in my young life yet. So when I say it was the paramedic who brought me back that is not quite true, in reality it was my curiosity of what I had left to do and the fact the Lord did not feel that it was my time to die yet. It was pure determination on my part, so I live my life as fully as I do.

CHAPTER 3

I am alive again: Indecision

When I arrived at the hospital by ambulance I was unconscious, my family was there and Mark's family was there. My father thought that since Mark and I had only been married five weeks, he felt like he raised me for seventeen years that he should have the say in what medical treatment I should receive. They had so many questions and so many decisions to make. They argued about who would make medical decisions for me, Mark or my father. Not sure if they brought the law into it but if they had of Mark would have won that war. My father offered Mark a way out of the marriage, he offered Mark an annulment. He didn't think Mark loved me enough to take care of me, or whether his mother would allow him to take care of me. My brothers were so upset with Mark that they had threatened to throw him out the window, and we were on the eighth floor. My father and Mark's mom argued about where I should have surgery. The decision was Mark's but his mother made all these important decisions, which were really Mark's decisions and this really upset my father. So Mark's mother decided I should get my surgery at a not too clean hospital and that's where I had it.

Surgery/Coma

The doctors had decided that I had brain damage, the doctor ordered a CAT scan. I was the first person in the Flint area who ever used a CAT scan to determine how serious the brain whiplash was. They performed a crainiotomy on me, which is a fancy word to say they opened my cranium and did brain surgery. What they found was not good. They found a sub dermal heme tome, which in layman's term is a blood clot in the brain caused by whiplash in the brain. I was sent to a different hospital for the surgery and I was there for about a week. While I was at this hospital I came down with a staph infection . My father was really upset, I went over to the hospital where I had surgery and I came back with a different sickness than when I went over to this hospital. When I returned to the the first hospital I was in, I returned to intensive care for a while in a coma. At first, when I was in intensive care, Mark was not allowed to see me since he had mononucleosis still, which is very contagious. After Mark was no longer contagious he was allowed into intensive care to see me. When he was allowed to see me, my lungs collapsed the first time he came in to see me. I was in a coma for five months, and the doctors didn't feel that I needed all this special care like physical therapy.

When I got out of intensive care Mark had arranged with the doctors what they called the closed-door policy, which meant that no one could enter my room while the door was closed without knocking. The doctors and Mark felt like I would come out of the coma quicker with my new husband showing me some intimacy. The doctors told my father and adopted mom that the left side of my brain was completely destroyed. At this time the doctors told my family and Mark that if I ever woke from the coma that I would never walk or talk again, and I would never have children and that I would be a vegetable. I spent years retraining the right side of my brain to do the job of the left side of my brain to do, like speaking. I not only spent years training my brain the job of speech but I taught it how to learn. I now only speak slowly with infliction where I used to have a monotone speech.

Aphasia

I was out of the coma, and I could understand every word spoken to me but I could not form verbal responses. On my 18th birthday I even remember blowing out my birthday candles, of course I had to be shown how and I didn't understand why. When I was in a half comatose stage Mark took me to use the bathroom and I recall him saying "sounds like Niagara Falls" and I giggled, this is when I believe I started my way back to family and loved ones. My family and loved ones didn't realize I was coming back.

I was aphasic, a fancy word that means I was unable to speak, I understood everything that was being said to me but I could not give a verbal reply to say I am here. It was like I was being held prisoner in my own body and I couldn't ask for help. Being aphasic was the longest period in my life, because as anyone who knows me now knows that talking to people is my life and without the ability to speak it is hard to let people know how important they are to you.

I was aphasic probably because the left side of my brain was totally destroyed and the left side of the brain controls your speech center. So before anyone knew I was out of the coma I had been transferring my speaking ability to the right side of my brain, how I did this I don't know! The doctors and nurses were really amazed and shocked. They had never had a patient with such ability and determination, but it wasn't really **my** ability that achieved this task, it was with God's help.

The first time I spoke, Mark, my husband, was the only one to hear me speak, and everyone said, " impossible you just want her to speak to relieve your guilt". When the nurses and doctors did realize I could speak they felt it was a miracle, so you see I am a walking miracle. Once it was evident to everyone that I was out of the coma the work began.

CHAPTER 4

The Long Journey Back

The sub dermal heme tome had the appearance of a stroke, the right half of my body was completely paralyzed, this made the journey back much more difficult. My right arm was pinned up against my chest and the therapist concentrated on this arm, they wanted to get it to go straight instead of pinned to my cheats. Now I can walk with my arm down at my side (although not straight), for a long time I couldn't even do that. To this day my right arm does not swing with my steps, my right arm does not swing freely. I was right handed so it was really hard for me to eat, but eating is a necessity of life so like retraining the right side of my brain to do things the left side of my brain did. I also trained myself to eat with my left hand. Although I could retrain myself to do all these things I could never train myself to write legibly with my left hand, but I guess that's because it was not a necessity of life.

Learning to tie my shoes was a real trip, and I couldn't take the easy way by getting slip on shoes because I needed to wear a knee- brace, which was built right into the shoe. The knee-brace was because I hyper- extended my right knee, so it wasn't just to learn to walk in the comfortable sneakers, but it was learning to walk with this big over-sized knee-brace. I had to learn to walk before they even thought about me going home from the hospital, and mind you I was never supposed to walk again. Kind of strange one of the one things I was never supposed to do again, I had to do before I was released from the hospital.

The last two weeks of high school days are completely gone. Because of the accident, I have no memory of this time at all. My ability to remember things that just happened or my short-term memory is pretty well shot. Even to this day my short-term memory is really bad, but it is so important that I can remember names. I have to repeat it twice to remember it. It is so important because I am such a people person and it shows respect to use a persons first name if you know it,

One thing that really irritated me is that they had to shave my hair off my head. I got so tired of strangers asking Mark "what's wrong with your little brother". I was aphasic and I couldn't put in my objection nor could I let them know I was not his little brother I was his wife. I finally did get my ability to speak back, but I was too polite to tell those who were calling me a boy what I thought of them.

MARK'S HOME

Mark and I had no place to live and once again Mark was without a job, so we did the only thing we could do and that was to move in with Mark's parents. This was a bad situation. We were allowed to occupy the whole basement. Now mind you I did not handle stairs real well, there was no railing on both sides of the staircase so I could either go up or down with no assistance. I could manage them with help but my in-laws were not willing to help. I was in Mark's life and they just wished I wasn't there in Mark's life at all. At this time Mark decided to go to school for his dream job, a police officer.

Mark's mother made me feel as if I were an anchor around Mark's neck. I remember calling up the stairs many times to see if Mark was home from school yet. I even remember Mark's mother saying Mark would have been better off without me. I remember thinking to myself she had wished I had died. All I wanted to do was to curl up and die. All I wanted was the man I had married, I wanted his love, and I wanted him to want me. He had married me to be his "trophy" wife, someone he could take to different events and say "see what I have, don't you wish you had her". It was evident I was no longer a wife he could have on his arm, I could barely walk and then it was with a limp, as he told me I was damaged goods or half a person.

I then realized the work I had to do was mine alone to do; I knew that with God's assistance I would recover, but you see the Lord helps those who help themselves and the Lords time does not always equal man's time. As it was it took 15 years to recover enough that I could go back to school (college),which was all I wanted to do to prove to myself I was not half a person. God works in mysterious ways, which is not always quick enough for me, so I really worked very hard towards recovery.

CHAPTER 5

Rehabilitation

Sometime in November I was admitted to rehabilitation hospital in Flint, Michigan where my rehabilitation began, It was a late beginning but at least it began. The staff was very pleasant and helpful. When I got to my room I found it was not a private room like at the first hospital I was in after the accident. I was very self-conscious about everything I did, like eating and speaking. Looking back on it now I can see why there were no private recovery rooms, their job was to get you used to doing all these different things in public.

I had two roommates that were two totally different types of people. There was a girl who was about twenty years old; she had the same kind of head injury that I had received. She had not been in a coma for as long as I was. She had her accident in June this was after I had debuted the CAT scan for the first time in Flint Michigan. I was really upset because she did not have to get her head shaved like I did. The second roommate was different in many ways. She was elderly, Chinese and she had not had an injury. She had a form of dementia, I think it was

Alzheimer, but this is before Alzheimer had been diagnosed.

All I could say is I want to go home, no matter what my home life was like, it was better than being in the hospital. So I spent six months in the rehabilitation hospital when they told me that there was nothing more they could do for me. I was told that normal house work would give me as much rehabilitation as they could give me.

CHAPTER 6

STARTING OVER

We returned home to Mark's parents home, where we resided for four months. After four months Mark felt that it was time he became an adult, he felt that as long as he was old enough to get married and go to college he was all grown up. So we moved to Davison, Michigan, into a downstairs studio apartment with the laundry facilities two buildings away. This was not the ideal apartment for a disabled wife, but it was not Mark's parents home, it was ours. We signed a month-to-month lease because we were unsure whether I would recover or would have to return to the hospital. We lived here for six months when we moved to a one-bedroom apartment, which was upstairs; the one bedroom was also in Davison. After living in Davison for two years, while Mark completed his associate degree in criminal justice, it was off to follow his dream in East Lansing, Michigan home of Michigan State University for Mark to complete his bachelors degree in criminal justice.

A NEW BEGINNING

I attempted to attend Michigan State University in 1978 but it was too soon. I only made it through one semester there. Mark had told me that community colleges were easier, so taking his advice I attended Lansing Community College. I attended this college for four years, a class or two a semester; I was still very damaged and was in need of a lot of help. Alas, as good as I was in high school, where I was ninth in my graduating class, I had not been through enough rehabilitation, so I gave up!

Mark did get his dream job that he had gone to school for, a Police Officer. He started working for Okemos Police Department, he got this job while he still had a year left for his Bachelors degree, he finished up his degree going to school in the evenings or what ever shift he was not working for that semester, because he was on rotating shifts. He was on the SWAT team while he was on Okemos police department.

I was happy in Lansing Michigan. We hired a builder to build our first house but the builder was taking draws of the money to build our house to build other houses, so our first house was a no-go, but I was not ready to give up.

CHAPTER 7

Another Beginning
Houston this time

The episode with the crooked builder started Mark thinking "The grass was always greener on the other side of the fence", Mark felt that he was wasting his education being a police officer so he felt his time would be better spent in a job that paid more money. So it was off to Houston, Texas where Mark tried becoming a 'head hunter', a person who looks for qualified people for certain jobs. Mark thought he could really make good money doing this, so much so that we rented a beautiful three-bedroom house.

Well reality set in, it took a whole two weeks for him to fall flat on his face, not a pretty sight. We lost the home we were renting, it was a rent-to-purchase good thing it was a month-to-month lease. Mark got a job as a store security guard in a department store, Joskies. We then moved to a one-bedroom apartment which was upstairs again, of course, Mark never took my disability in to account for anything. Stairs were still not my friend.

It was at this time that I started to gain weight, fear that I might be pregnant started to set in. I was five months pregnant before I ever went to a free clinic for a pregnancy test, the test came back positive and all Mark could say is that I thought we had agreed that we would never have children, which really devastated me. I felt like once again I was a disappointment to Mark and our marriage, just like the disability was something that was thrown on him thru no fault of his own. In reality it was not me who was doing the disappointment, it was Mark. It was Mark who was at fault for the accident, which caused my disability, and it was Mark who had gotten me pregnant.

Mark really felt like he was not using his education as a store security guard at which time he felt that being a police officer was not so bad. It was at that time that Mark applied for the Houston Police Department. He felt that he was sure to get on the department because of his education but it was a disappointing blow when he was turned away. So he applied for the Harris County Sheriff department, where he was gladly accepted, they loved him having the education.

A NEW BEGINNING

After my daughter was born we decided to try our

hand at building a home again, it was really because we had a child that we decided to try building another home. This time we had real success. We had a three-bedroom home in a wonderful family oriented neighborhood with no stairs, on a cul-de-sac so our back yard was huge. The neighbors were great, and they accepted me as a person in spite of my disability. I was four months pregnant for my daughter before I ever realized I was pregnant, pretty strange seeing how I was never suppose to be able to have children because of the accident. My daughter Kandy Marie was born on November 6, 1982.

It was three months after my daughter was born, I was pregnant again. The second pregnancy you get big a lot quicker or so I thought. I went to the doctor and he says congratulations its twins, I was excited until Mark found out, Mark proceeded to say, "Anything I plan never works out, I planned to have two kids not three". Alas I lost these twins when I was five and a half months pregnant. I was too large to fit behind the steering wheel to drive. The twin boys were stillborn at five and a half months and they were huge when they were stillborn. One weighed three and a half pounds and the other twin weighed one and a half pound.

The doctor told Mark to get me pregnant again as quickly as possible, so I would not have time to think about the loss. So I lost the twins in August and I was pregnant again by October. I was worried with this pregnancy. Every little pain it was off to the hospital I would go. So I had four false labors with my son Kristopher Allan. When Kristopher was born, because I had had four false labors the doctor was in no hurry, so he is putting his gloves on telling me to blow and out popped Kristopher's head. Now the size of Kristopher could have been the reason for the false labors because he was so large, nine pounds six ounces, Kandy was eight pounds and two ounces, they were big babies. But you know what they say about Texas "every thing comes big in Texas"! and they were born in Texas. We lived in Houston for four full summers and I was pregnant for three of them. I started to tell people who came to visit us that "if you don't want to get pregnant while in Houston, you don't drink the water". I call my children 'Miracle' babies', they have been the sunshine of my life. Showing me that all things are possible.

CHAPTER 8

Another Adventure

After enduring the heat of Houston. Mark once again came up with the idea of the grass being greener on the other side of the fence. This time although I must give him credit he at least checked it out first. He checked it out job wise, and we even took a vacation there. We made it our ten-year anniversary trip. Our anniversary was in April, so there was snow in the mountains. Mark and I had seen snow before but our two little children had not. The first time my daughter saw snow she reached down to pick it up and said "oh, yucky!". That was her first experience with snow but not her last, now she is an avid snowboarder, a far cry from the four year old that thought snow was 'yucky'.

Mark had always wanted to live in the Rocky Mountain region ever since the years he spent in the Air Force. He did ask my thoughts on it this time. I loved Mark very much and if it would make him happy I was happy. I am very happy at this point in my life in Colorado and very thankful that Mark had wandering feet, and an itch that nothing could satisfy until we reached Colorado.

So in the summer of 1986 we moved up to Longmont, Colorado into a townhouse. The townhouse was nice but it was a far cry from our three-bedroom house in Houston, it was way too small after experiencing a full three-bedroom home.

So as a police officer Mark worked rotating shifts which rotated every three months. We tried to join in on all the different activities, as much as I could. We played volleyball once a week; we got mountain bikes and rode them, although I was not too good uphill. I tried to go back to school to a community college twelve years after the accident, but I was unable to do it, I felt like such a failure.

CHAPTER 9

The Big Boo-Boo

I had spent the last 13 years recovering from the accident when I felt like I was well enough to get a job. I was lucky and I got a job as a child day care worker at the YMCA in Longmont. Where I worked for two years. At which point I decided I could do more than this. I did great in high school, so good that my senior year they passed me without taking a single final and there is the fact that I was voted most likely to succeed out of my high school class. So I researched all the universities in the area for the university that would give me the most assistance (with my disability I need a lot of assistance), and I found it. The winner was Northern Colorado University in Greeley, Colorado. I also wanted my two children to see how important I felt it was to go as far as you can in education. I started at Northern Colorado University in 1993. I was hesitant about starting because I knew that Mark would see that I was no longer as dependent as I once was.

Mark had four different affairs on me in the seventeen years we were married and I forgave him for each and every one of them. But after the fourth affair, he said to me "how can you forgive me for these affairs, if it were you I would never forgive you". I then replied to him "don't worry I will not forgive you again". Mark had told me repeatedly that no man would ever love me, I was half a woman and that I was damaged goods, I took all this verbal abuse and yet he did not understand that I loved him deeply.

I remember the day my love fell out of my life. It was 1994, when I was attending a night class, I came home from class, Mark was watching our two children when all of a sudden out of nowhere he says to me "I can't put up with this shit". I asked him what was wrong, he says to me "I have only stayed with you for so long cause I felt guilty". I replied to him "don't let the door hit you in the ass on the way out, I don't need anyone's guilt". Even though I was hurt I have always put my children first. I made sure he went in and told his children good-bye. I endured this verbal abuse for the life of the marriage because he was my husband and I did love him.

It took almost a year and a half for my divorce from Mark because he fought me the whole way. Looking back on it now I can see what was right in front of my face. Mark's affairs were his cry to get out of this marriage and I was to close to see it. I see it now and I hold no bad feelings towards him, after all he gave me my children.

CHAPTER 10

The Bigger Boo-Boo

I was married when I was 17 and I was unaware of how to find men to date so, I joined a dating service. I was in my second year of college when I married Donald, although I found it very difficult concentrating while I was going through the divorce from Mark. This is where my desire to show my children how important I felt an education was, and I am not a quitter.

After being told for so many years that I would never have another man to love me by Mark, I was overwhelmed by the feeling of being unworthy of a man's love. So the first man that said, "I love you" was the man I took to the altar. So the second husband was a rebound husband. I told myself that I loved Donald, my second husband. We got married in Las Vegas where we enjoyed a weekend in. Shortly after we were married Donald became very physically abusive. After we were married I found out that Donald was gay too, he had married me to prove to his family that he was not gay.

Abuse had become a way of life for me, although it was physical abuse now. With Mark it had always been verbal, you see Mark was a police officer and he knew that marks were evidence. Even though this abuse was of a different nature, I would have taken it but Derrick's one mistake was that he started to turn his abuse to my children. I remained married to Donald for four years that is when his abuse had a different target. This divorce took a lot less time to finalize, this was because we had less time together. After my marriage to Donald, a physically abusive man was over, I made a promise to myself; no man would ever touch me out of anger again!

CHAPTER 11

A FAIRY TALE

Once I had met husband number three, Daniel, I thought he was the one. I am not a person who is materialistic, but I am a person who had been living paycheck to paycheck, so when I met Daniel and he started to lavish me with all types of extravagant gifts I thought he really loved me. Being a person who was not raised having all the money you could ever possibly want or need I was not used to this life. I had met David in April and by June he had asked me to marry him, but because I had only known Mark for four months before I married him and Derrick one month I decided that I would make it a year engagement, besides that I wanted to see my daughter graduate from the high school she had gone to for four years.

I did have a wedding that was very memorable; I guess you could call it a fairy tale wedding. I was under the impression that because my prior two marriages had been done via elopement and not in a church, this was the reason for my divorces.

So I was married in a church for marriage three. Daniel

supplied everything including my wedding dress. He bought dresses for my bridesmaids and maid of honor, the tuxes for the men; he even had all the ladies hair done. He supplied the money for all these things. It was my ideas to make the reception potluck, although a potluck alone was not show enough for him, he needed to hire a disc jockey and a photographer. We had the wedding in Niwot, Colorado, and then walked down to the church where the reception was held. we only walked to another church because that church had an elevator to the basement. We spent our wedding night playing pinochle. We played until three in the morning, yet ,we had to catch a flight to Cancun at nine in the morning.

It was Daniel who brought me back to the church which I had was hesitant about getting involved in one again because I was blaming God for the accident, I realize now that God had nothing to do with it. He was the one who gave me the determination to get thru it. Daniel I thought I really loved him, that is the only reason I would allow myself to be taken away from my home and children and be taken to California.

Daniel worked at IBM in Gunbarrell, Colorado for the first 2 years of our marriage until the year 2003 at which time he had 30 years in the company. So he got his retirement. But money was so important to him so he got a job out in California, Rancho Bernardo was the city in California. He worked for this company that was based out of California in Longmont for about six months at which point we moved to California. We lived in a temporary housing situation for the first three months, then we moved to Escondido. I thought that I would have no trouble fitting in, after all the adventures I had been on with Mark but low and behold, you had to live in California your whole life to be accepted as one of them. We moved into a beautiful house with four different levels, I was concerned of so many sets of stairs. But I have always tried to make my man happy so I didn't fight him about getting a house with no stairs but stairs still were not my friend so I fell down each set of stairs at least twice. This home also had an outdoor kitchen, a underground swimming pool and a spa. All of this was to show that Daniel was sitting so high on the money market. This house made Daniel very happy so I tried to be happy too.

Time passed, I constantly tried to make new friends that's just me. As the time passed we got so we were constantly arguing about something or other. I got into great physical condition for me, I had got into the habit of walking five miles at each occurrence of an argument, and they were abundant. We got into many arguments but he **knew** that I would not be physically abused again.

In April 2006, Daniel had taken a business trip to Denver from California and while he was in Colorado he suffered a stroke. The doctors had told Daniel the best way to prevent another stroke would be by losing some of his weight. So I very consciously helped him lose 50 pounds in two months. After he had lost this weight in June 2006 he asked me for a divorce. Now mind you, Daniel had had a stroke, he was a completely different person after that stroke. He told me that he had asked me to marry him so that I would go to Hawaii with him. You see he had a time- share there. I think he expected me to roll over and accept the divorce, because that is what his first wife did. I didn't, I immediately went down to see an attorney. This visit to the attorney was well worth it, I found out that I would receive $4200 dollars in alimony a month. I told Daniel this, he did not believe me he had to check with his lawyer and when he found out the amount I had quoted him was correct he pulled the divorce off the table.

We had three very stressful years after that. Daniel got a transfer which brought us back to Colorado, I was still struggling to make our marriage work, but at least I was at home.

CHAPTER 12

Be true to thyself

We moved to Colorado in January 2010 where we lived in a temporary housing situation for about three months, during these three months we were actively looking at real estate. I wanted to move back to Greeley where my children and grandchildren were living, but Daniel said no! So we concentrated on a new development called Reunion, which was in Commerce City. I would say we were happy but I was not, I was so unhappy that I went for a drive in the mountains, and I have always been afraid that I would hurt myself because I do not handle curves in the mountains too good. Daniel was happy because he was going to have his daughter come live with us. We had it all planned out Dan and I would fly to the DC area and Daniel would drive the U-haul back with his daughter and grandson and I would fly home with his granddaughter. Well time got closer and his daughter calls and tells me that she has an interview for a job on Wednesday. All the time his daughter was thinking about coming to live with us I tried to impress on her that I would not be a built in babysitter.

So Daniel and I had a small argument over this, and he got very upset at this point. He got upset enough that he threw me into a house plant yelling at me that "you're not even family". At this point I said, "I might as well go out and drive at night and kill myself, it would be cheaper than a divorce". I am no fool I do not drive at night because I cannot see at night. So I am parked in front of a convenience store and I get a knock on my car window, it's a police officer. The police officer says "we've been looking for you". I said "because I'm so sweet?" He tells me no your husband called and said you were going to hurt yourself. I explained to them exactly what had happened, they said I had two choices either go to the hospital with these paramedics voluntarily and they would probably let you go tonight or we will take you in and you will have to stay three days. I said I will go voluntarily. After they strapped me in the officer steps into the ambulance and says we want you to sign this complaint, we're going over to arrest your husband. I said if I don't sign it you will not arrest him, but they said "no ma'am we are going over to arrest him anyway" so I spent five hours in the hospital and he spent five days in jail.

After his little episode of pushing me around I divorced him because I had told Daniel that I would never allow another man to touch me out of anger, so the divorce should not have been any surprise to him. Once again I was without a companion. I do not do good without a companion.

CHAPTER 13

Alone Again?

I was alone, without a companion for approximately five months, when I bumped into Charles on a dating site. We officially met at Starbucks, pretty strange for a person who can't stand the taste of coffee to meet a potential companion in a Starbucks coffee house, but that's where you meet most of these online dates for, coffee. Charles seemed like the answer to my prayers. He seemed like a loving understanding individual.

We met a Starbucks and Charles wanted to take me on a date to Black Hawk. Which would have been fine but I had driven to Starbucks from my apartment and I didn't want to leave my car in Starbucks parking lot. So we discussed it and we decided that Charles would follow me to my apartment, he did not know where I lived. I was not used to anyone following me. Well at the entrance to Starbucks is a traffic light so I turned left at the traffic light while it was turning red. Charles did not make it through the light, he was unable to find where I had driven to. We both were quite upset, we had really though we had a love connection. So I checked my computer when I got home, so fearful that I had found a love connection and my crazy driving had caused me to lose him. But when I checked my computer there was an e-mail there with his phone number, and of course I called it.

The first date we went on was a date up to Black Hawk, a town up in the mountains which is a gambling community. Charles showed me a lot of care and concern in regards to my disability. Charles showed me things that I was led to believe I could never do. Charles had a Harley Davidson motorcycle, which I really thought I could never ride on, because my first husband had tore down my confidence in doing things, after all I was damaged goods. But I enjoyed it so much, I thought I would be scared but I wasn't. So I can thank Charles for help me rebuild my confidence up.

Our first motorcycle ride we went to old town Fort Collins in Colorado, and we went to the Anheuser Bush brewery. We then returned and stopped at my daughters house. I told Charles that my daughter would think he is corrupting me,- a biker girl and drinking beer. Our first motorcycle trip was a 3500 mile trip down to Texas, where we went through Raton Pass to Dallas to visit my adopted mom. We then continued on to San Antonio, then on to Fredricksburg finally we made it to our destination in Austin to the Republic of Texas motorcycle rally. On our drive home to Greeley we ran into a town that was dealing with forest fires around it, the town was Raton Pass. We ended up spending the night at a Comfort Inn in Raton Pass and we had to take another route home, which made the trip longer.

I really had a great time on all the trips that Charles took me on. In October of 2011 Charles had given me a Ruby ring, I was so excited because I thought this was the beginning. The beginning of always having a man by my side for the rest of my life.

CHAPTER 14

Reality

I had what I thought was a love connection with Charles for almost two years (1 month short of 2 years). When I had first met Charles he had been divorced for 15 years. In one breath he tells me that he thinks a couple who has been together for two years should get married and then in his next breath he tells me that he will never get married again, he will just rent a wife. I thought this was cute until the two year mark approached, all the care and concern had left the relationship. I gave him his ring back and told him that I did not think he was serious enough and whenever he did get more serious he could give it back to me. Alas he never did get more serious. He even started to blame me for his financial circumstances. He told me that he had spent $32,000 on me but it was not on me. What he had spent the money on was a camper to go on his truck and a three wheel motorcycle. Why do I give my heart so freely, without worry, unconditionally?

CHAPTER 15

OOPS: Again Bad Decision Reboundy

It was the same month I had broken up with Charles that I found Cleto, husband #4. We met at Starbucks, he said I was 30 minutes late, being a 20 year retired Navy vet and a 23 year nurse told me I was lucky he waited for me, but looking back on it now, was it really "lucky". We had only known each other 10 months when we walked down the aisle in my backyard. He wanted me to sell my home and buy a RV so we could travel the United States. I said no. I told him I wanted some place to come home to, and that if anything ever happened to him I could not drive it. Then we had taken a trip to Rocky Mountain National Park. In between Loveland and Fort Collins, he saw houses for rent and he said "wouldn't you love to live here", and I said "not in your wildest dreams". He constantly tried to change me; who I was and how I dealt with other people.

I remember 4th of July when we went over to some bowling buddies home for celebration picnic, we are seated with the bowling buddy that I do all my bowling with and I consider a close friend. Cleto has the nerve to ask her "if Mary lost both of her arms would you give her one of yours?". This just floored me. After the picnic, on our drive home I asked him what right he had asking her that. He told me that if she were any type of friend she would have said yes and that is how he measures friendship. I told him what kind of friend would I be to disable one of my good friends. I think this is when he finally realized I was not going to change for him or no man, he took the next step.

Then in July (my birthday month) he approached me and said "I am not happy, I want a divorce". He had said I want to give you something I know no one else can give you for your birthday, I will give you a divorce. On August 1, 2014 we went down to the court and signed the divorce papers, they told us that the divorce will be final November 3 and he said an early Christmas present for you too. We signed the papers and I was crying, no emotions from him. I guess it is only fitting, we knew each other for 10 months before we married, that our marriage lasted only 10 months. I feel like such a failure sometimes. I had really felt like this was the man that God wanted me to marry, who am I to argue with God, obviously it was the devil who made me do it. I couldn't believe I had made the same mistake as I made with husband number two; I had not learned from a previous mistake, a total rebound again. Will I ever learn?

CHAPTER 16

BUDDIES

Looking at my life history, not being able to find a man who could accept me for who I am and what I have to offer them, the fact that I am such a people person. I came to a realization that maybe the job of loving me is too great for one man. Maybe I am meant to live my life without a mate, this is not my choice though. I would say alone, but I have so many friends I am never alone.

I have met a man named Dennis, we have agreed that we will be buddies, but I think I love him and he says he loves me too. I am scared I have not had the best luck with men. Dennis says that he is a one woman at a time man. Dennis was married to the same woman for 30 years. I think I could really have a serious relationship with him if I were not so scared. I have been emotionally hurt by men in the past who have told me I love you. My heart seems to be an open target for men to hit the bulls-eye and the bulls eye they hit injures me emotionally. I would say it ruins my self esteem, but I have many friends to rescue me from having my self esteem destroyed. Besides that, I must say that my self esteem is quite high. It has to be with all I have gone through in my life. My will to live is strong as well as my zest for life. I don't think I will ever marry again just be real good buddies with Dennis, but them again time will tell.

Confusion

I was confused about which man I should be with Charles (Charles is the previous man who said he will rent a wife) or Dennis. As Charles was not attached, he had broken up with his girlfriend. Being the kind of woman I am, I could not lead Dennis on because at this time I thought I still had feelings for Charles. On New Years Eve Charles spent with me, we reminisced about the two years we had spent together looking at all my magnets which represents all the places we had been together, plus we were bowling together in two different leagues a couple times a week. So I felt like he may want to get back together with me. I had asked Charles if he thought there was a possibility of us getting back together and he said he needs to ask the girl he broke up with if she wanted him.

I helped Charles celebrate his 62 birthday on Sunday February 1 and then on February 3, his official birthday. We went up to Black Hawk, while we were there Charles was texting on his phone constantly. All I can figure is he must have been texting the girl who broke up with him because when we were on the way home he really got angry with me and used some really inappropriate language (f---king) this and that. I was totally appalled, I had never heard this kind of language from him.

I thought maybe Charles and I could still make a go of it. Charles even invited me to go to visit his friend Allen with him. This was like waving a flag in my face saying maybe. Then he asked me to go on a motorcycle trip down to the Republic of Texas rally he said it would be like us reliving the past. Alas Texas had a lot of rain the summer of 2015 and Charles thought the ground would be too wet to camp out so instead we took a trip west. We started out going to Grand Canyon, where they had an observation deck. The stairs up to the observation deck were too steep for me to handle so Charles went up by himself, I have never limited any man I have been with because of my disability.

When we got to Las Vegas Charles felt that it was too hot to stay in his little camper so we rented a room in one of the casinos. We walked all around the casino the first night and did some gambling. The second night we walked up and down the Las Vegas strip, which is not really far,but with my disability it's a lot. Then after doing all this walking Charles wants me to walk down to Harley Davidson motorcycle dealer, which was a couple of miles off the strip. I told him I don't think I can make the trip, so he drops me off in a casino and tells me he would pick me up when he gets back. This is a far cry from the concern he had for me at one time.

We then proceeded on our trip to the west coast, we stopped at a restaurant near San Diego and I asked Charles why he had the VW bug, before he told me he was going to sell the bug. His response was "I wanted a vehicle Peggy would be safe in". I commented "you don't care if I'm safe." Then all hell broke loose and Charles said to me I'll just take you to San Diego and buy you a ticket and send you home. Well we got to Escondido where I used to live and he said you want to camp here, but I was so hurt I just wanted to go home. Besides that no man has the right to threaten me. So call me a fool, but I thought maybe we could make a go until then.

Dennis understood about my confusion, he never faltered from his love for me. I think another reason for the break-up between Dennis and I was that his divorce was not final yet. His divorce was final on February 13, I felt like now I could pursue him. After his divorce was finalized I noticed his ex-wife had taken Dennis to the cleaners. Dennis had always tried to do everything for his family. Therefore he was thousands of dollars in debt, and because he was so far in debt he had to work all this over-time which left no time for me. I felt like I was being put on the back burner, I don't like that position. So we broke up for a while until I heard a good sermon from my pastor which told me struggling makes you the person God wants you to be, which I realized was true because of all the struggling I have done for the past 39 years. After hearing this sermon I came to the realization that not all people struggle over the same thing. I struggle over my romantic life, while Dennis struggles over his financial life. I have told him I can assist him to manage his finances better, and he has vowed to help me with my romantic life. Yet I am still scared, should I venture in? I guess I will as friends.

As of February 15 2016 Dennis's job with the Railroad station in Denver had all the employees who had any type of seniority move to North Platte Nebraska, so it was good bye to Dennis.

ANOTHER TRY

Charles was on my mind still, he had never left my mind. Charles was still bowling with me, he had never lost sight of me. It took a little time but he realizes that he does still love me, my love for him has never stopped

I am writing this story to show others what sure determination can bring you in life with help from the almighty. This life story is not saying your life will be perfect. As you can see by all the mistakes I have made, but sure determination has made it possible for me to be here to make these mistakes. Thank you for visiting my book, I hope this assist you in any struggles you may be going through.